The Morristown &
Morris Township Library

1 Miller Road
Morristown NJ 07960

It's a Baby
Black Bear!

Kelly Doudna

Consulting Editor, Diane Craig, M.A./Reading Specialist

ABDO
Publishing Company

Published by ABDO Publishing Company, 8000 West 78th Street, Edina, Minnesota 55439.

Copyright © 2008 by Abdo Consulting Group, Inc. International copyrights reserved in all countries.

No part of this book may be reproduced in any form without written permission from the publisher. SandCastle™ is a trademark and logo of ABDO Publishing Company.

Printed in the United States.

Editor: Pam Price
Content Developer: Nancy Tuminelly
Cover and Interior Design and Production: Mighty Media
Photo Credits: AbleStock, Peter Arnold Inc. (P. Henry, Steven Kazlowski, Bruce Lichtenberger, Lynn Rogers, Carl R. Sams II, R. Wittek)

Library of Congress Cataloging-in-Publication Data

Doudna, Kelly, 1963-
  It's a baby black bear! / Kelly Doudna.
     p. cm. -- (Baby mammals)
  ISBN 978-1-60453-023-0
  1. Black bear--Juvenile literature. 2. Black bear--Infancy--Juvenile literature. I. Title.

QL737.C27D67 2008
599.78'5139--dc22
                              2007033740

SandCastle™ would like to hear from you. Please send us your comments and suggestions.
sandcastle@abdopublishing.com

Vital Statistics

for the Black Bear

BABY NAME
cub

NUMBER IN LITTER
1 to 4, average 2 or 3

WEIGHT AT BIRTH
8 to 12 ounces

AGE OF INDEPENDENCE
1½ years

ADULT WEIGHT
125 to 500 pounds

LIFE EXPECTANCY
15 to 25 years

Black bear cubs are born during winter. They stay in the den with their mother until spring.

Black bear cubs are born blind and with very little hair.

A black bear mother is called a sow. She raises her cubs alone. A father bear is called a boar. He does not help raise the cubs.

Black bears are omnivores. They eat twigs, berries, nuts, and insects. Sometimes they also eat fish and small mammals.

An omnivore eats everything, including both plants and meat.

Black bears live mostly in forests and shrubby areas. They also live in wetlands.

Sows communicate with cubs using woofs and grunts. A cub's cries sound a lot like those of a human baby!

Black bears have few enemies in the wild. But in Florida alone, more than 100 black bears are killed each year by cars.

When a sow senses danger, she sends her cubs up the nearest tree.

Black bears come down trees backward, often falling the last few feet!

Cubs grow rapidly. They weigh 30 to 60 pounds by the time they're one year old.

Young bears leave their mothers when they are about one-and-a-half years old.

Fun Fact
About the Black Bear

Black bears walk with a flat-footed shuffle. But they have been clocked running at speeds over 30 miles per hour. That's faster than a champion sprinter!

Glossary

clock – to measure the speed at which something travels.

communicate – to share ideas, information, or feelings.

den – a small hollow used by an animal for shelter.

expectancy – an expected or likely amount.

independence – the state of no longer needing others to care for or support you.

omnivore – one who eats both meat and plants.

shuffle – to walk without picking up one's feet.

wetland – a low, wet area of land such as a swamp or a marsh.

To see a complete list of SandCastle™ books and other nonfiction titles from ABDO Publishing Company, visit **www.abdopublishing.com**.

8000 West 78th Street, Edina, MN 55439

800-800-1312 • 952-831-1632 fax